Love Never Fails
120 Reflections

DEBRA HERBECK

Cover design by Mary Ann Smith
Book design by Mark Sullivan

ISBN 978-1-61636-530-1

Published by Servant Books, an imprint of
Franciscan Media
28 W. Liberty St.
Cincinnati, OH 45202
www.FranciscanMedia.org

Printed in the United States of America.
Printed on acid-free paper.
13 14 15 16 17 5 4 3 2 1

This book is dedicated to my father, Jacob, whose whole life was characterized by generosity, selflessness, and loving care. You gave me the two most precious gifts—life and love—and I am eternally grateful. You will be greatly missed, but your legacy of love continues on.

Foreword
—*by Jennifer Fulwiler*

Love: It would be almost impossible for a society to be more confused about the meaning of this word than ours is today.

Sometimes it's hard to know what true, Christlike love looks like in the hustle and bustle of daily life: How do you love yourself without becoming selfish? How do you serve your loved ones with all your heart, yet avoid pushing yourself to the point of spiritual or physical exhaustion? What does it mean to show love to that guy who won't let you merge when you're trying to get onto the highway in traffic? Every Christian will face questions like these at some point or another; Some of us struggle with them every day.

This is why *Love Never Fails: 120 Reflections* is the perfect resource for our times. In this culture where confusion about love is rampant both in society at large and in the individual human heart, Debbie Herbeck has compiled an invaluable collection of wisdom. St. Francis de Sales, Catherine de Hueck Doherty, Pope John Paul II, and countless other spiritual luminaries act as guides to help us navigate this troubled territory.

Mother Teresa of Calcutta tells us what it looks like for a saint to love her neighbors (quote #36), and St. Augustine of Hippo offers a warning about when love veers into idolatry (quote #112). Henri J.M. Nouwen explains what love looks like in friendship (quote #17), and C.S. Lewis describes what it looks like in marriage (quote #53). St. Thérèse of the Child Jesus reminds us that love is so much more than just a feeling (quote #3), and Cardinal Donald Wuerl tells us that if it doesn't begin and end with God, it's not real love at all (quote #44).

By the end of the book, you'll feel as though you've been led through a wilderness of temptation and sin and gently steered onto the path of true love, forged by Christ himself.

The *Catechism* teaches that "the fundamental and innate vocation of every human is to love" (quote #35), and this is a book to turn to again and again as each of us fights the daily battle to live out that call more perfectly in our lives.

Introduction

I am not a romantic, I'm a realist, and yet I think about love all the time. Love is what gives my life direction and purpose. Love shapes my actions and guides my words; it gets me out of bed in the morning and helps me sleep at night. Love tells me who I am and helps me see others as they really are.

Love is real. At the center of this reality is a divine Person, the source of all human love whose outstretched arms show me what true love looks like. This immense love is deeper and wider than the whole universe, yet it stoops low to enter my poor soul and ignite a flame within me that will burn forever.

Real love is necessary for real life. Real love shows up not only in times of great joy, delight, and fulfillment, but especially when life seems overwhelming and incomprehensible, filled with unbearable suffering and sorrow. It is in these times that love has shown me the way, not around the pain, but through it. Love is stronger than death.

Many years ago I asked God to fill me with his love and teach me what it truly means to love. Every day I try to say yes to loving the person God gives me in that moment—my husband, a family member, a friend, a coworker, a stranger, an adversary, even myself. If I can string together these moments of love, then perhaps my life can be a reflection of God's great love.

It is difficult for me to express in words the true meaning of love, but it is even harder to live it—not just in short intervals, but day in and day out. Perhaps that's why in this book, I've chosen those who have completed their journey towards love or are well on their way, to help point the way to the One who is Love. My prayer is that their words about love, and even more importantly their lives of love, will inspire you as they have me, to say Yes to Love, each moment of every day.

The
Quotes

1 | GOD IS ON YOUR SIDE

Do not fear God, for perfect love casts out fear. God is biased in your favor. Would you rather be judged by the justice of the peace of your town on the last day, or by the King of Peace? Most certainly by God, would you not? God is more lenient than you because he is perfectly good and, therefore, loves you more. Be bold enough, then, to believe that God is on your side, even when you forget to be on His. Live your life, then, not by law, but by love. As Augustine said, "Love God and then do whatever you please." If you love God, you will never do anything to hurt God, and, therefore, never make yourself unhappy.

—*Fulton J. Sheen*

2 | PROTECTING YOUR HEART

To love at all is to be vulnerable. Love anything, and your heart will certainly be wrung and possibly be broken. If you want to make sure of keeping it intact, you must give your heart to no one, not even to an animal. Wrap it carefully round with hobbies and little luxuries, avoid all entanglements; lock it up safe in the casket or coffin of your selfishness. But in that casket—safe, dark, motionless, airless—it will change. It will not be broken; it will become unbreakable, impenetrable, irredeemable. The alternative to tragedy, or at least to the risk of tragedy, is damnation. The only place outside Heaven where you can be perfectly safe from all the dangers and perturbations of love is Hell. ...Christ did not teach and suffer that we might become, even in the natural loves, more careful of our own happiness... We shall draw nearer to God not by trying to avoid the sufferings inherent in our lives, but by accepting them and offering them to him; throwing away all defensive armor. If our hearts need to be broken, and if he chooses this as the way in which they should break, so be it.

—C.S. Lewis

3 | LOVE IS NOT A FEELING

I reminded myself that charity isn't a matter of fine sentiments; it means doing things. So I determined to treat this sister as if she were the person I loved best in the world. Every time I met her, I used to pray for her, offering to God all her virtues and her merits.

—St. Thérèse of the Child Jesus

4. | JESUS WAITS TO TELL YOU

The devil may try to use the hurts of life, and sometimes our own mistakes to make you feel it is impossible that Jesus really loves you…. This is a danger for all of us. And so sad, because it is completely the opposite of what Jesus is really wanting, waiting to tell you. Not only that he loves you, but even more—he longs for you. He misses you when you don't come close. He thirsts for you. He loves you always, even when you don't feel worthy. When not accepted by others, even by yourself sometimes, he is the one who always accepts you. Only believe—you are precious to him. Bring all your suffering to his feet—only open your heart to be loved by him as you are. He will do the rest.

—*Mother Teresa of Calcutta*

5 | TRUE PURPOSE

O you who were created for union of love with God himself and whom he is ever attracting to himself, what are you doing with your precious lives, with your time? You are laboring for nothingness and all you think you possess is pure misery. O terrible human blindness. So great a light about you and you do not see it! So clear a voice sounding and you do not hear!

—*St. John of the Cross*

6 | How Love Is Judged

The most trivial work, the least action when inspired by love, is often of greater merit than the most outstanding achievement. It is not on our face value that God judges our deeds, even when they bear the stamp of apparent holiness, but solely on the measure of love we put into them.

—*St. Thérèse of the Child Jesus*

7 | COURAGE TO LOVE

...The greatest romance we will ever experience is God's passionate love. The greatest adventure is the journey into his kingdom. The greatest achievement is to live as a faith-filled brother or sister of Jesus, the Savior. The greatest challenge is to carry on Jesus' mission and ministry, incarnating his healing presence and saving love in the world. Through our love for one another, others will experience Immanuel—the fact that God is, indeed, with us. This means that you and I will have to become the hands and arms of God's love in our world by reaching out to the suffering and marginal people of this metropolitan area, of our nation, of the world. We have to be willing to let the indwelling of God's love move us into courageous and creative service and ministry.

—Cardinal Joseph Bernardin

8 | WHAT THE WORLD NEEDS NOW

The whole world needs to hear two things with strength and power: "God loves you" and "I love you." You must say it often to your friends. This world isn't starving from a lack of money. It's starving from a want of love.

—Mother Angelica

9 | THE FRIENDSHIP OF JESUS

Jesus is your Friend—*the* friend—with a human heart, like yours, with most loving eyes that wept for Lazarus. And as much as he loved Lazarus, he loves you...

—St. Josemaría Escrivá

10 | Love Without Measure

Lord, may I have balance and measure in everything—
except in Love.

—St. Josemaría Escrivá

11 | Leaning into Love

When we are linked by the power of prayer, we as it
were, hold each other's hand as we walk side by side
along a slippery path; and thus by the bounteous
disposition of charity, it comes about that the harder
each one leans on the other, the more firmly we are
riveted together in brotherly love.

—St. Gregory the Great

12 | PASSIONATE LOVE AFFAIR

The greatest tragedy of our world is that men do not know, really know, that God loves them. Some believe it in a shadowy sort of way. If they were to really think about it they would soon realize that their belief in God's love for them is very remote and abstract.

Because of this lack of realization of God's love for them, men do not know how to love God back. Often they don't even try, because it all seems so very difficult, and so very, very remote…

Christians must also realize, with a joy that can scarcely be expressed, that the Christian faith, in its essence, is a love affair between God and man.

Not just a *simple* love affair: It is a *passionate* love affair. God so loved man that he created him in his image. God so loved man that he became man himself, died on a cross, was raised from the dead by the Father, ascended into heaven—and all this in

order to bring man back to himself, to that heaven which he had lost through his own fault…Where love is, God is.

—Catherine de Hueck Doherty

13 | WIDOW'S MITE

Even if we do not have at our disposal riches and concrete capacities to meet the needs of our neighbors, we cannot feel dispensed from opening our hearts to their necessities and relieving them as far as possible. Remember the widow's mite. She threw into the treasury of the temple only two small coins, but with them, all her great love…. It is, above all, the interior value of the gift that counts: the readiness to share everything, the readiness to give oneself. St. Paul writes: "If I give away all my possessions… but do not have love, I gain nothing."

—Pope John Paul II

14 | THE MEANING OF EVERYTHING

Not only is love everything, but everything is love. Love is the soul of everything valuable. The most precious gift in the world given without love is worthless; the cheapest gift in the world given with love is priceless.... Everything valuable is *made of* love. Everything that exists, from yourself to a grain of sand, is God's love made visible, made incarnate—love in the form of creation. The words He spoke to create everything in the universe—"let it be"—were the words of love.... History is God's love drama. Matter is love's body. Gravity is love's energy when it moves not souls but stars and stones and storms. We are love's children.... Your very existence is God's love of you. Love is the meaning of life and the meaning of religion and the meaning of everything.

—*Peter Kreeft*

15 | GENUINE LOVE

Where love is genuine, it has got to be shown, not with words, but with the reality and daily acts of our life.... When love is based on gratitude at knowing oneself loved and forgiven, the soul will never be at a loss as to how to express such love, through every word, thought, and deed, but especially through a habitual silence that just wants to admire and adore.

—Erasmo Leiva-Merikakas

16 | A RESTING PLACE

We find rest in those we love, and we provide a resting place in ourselves for those who love us.

—St. Bernard of Clairvaux

17 | DARE TO LOVE

Friendship becomes more and more possible when you accept yourself as deeply loved. Then you can be with others in a non-possessive way. Real friends find their inner correspondence where both know the love of God. There spirit speaks to spirit and heart to heart.

True friendships are lasting because true love is eternal.... Love between people, when given by God, is stronger than death. When you have loved deeply, that love can grow even stronger after the death of the person you love.... You have to trust that every true friendship has no end, that a communion of saints exists among all those, living and dead, who have truly loved God and one another. You know from experience how real this is. Those you have loved deeply and who have died live on in you, not just as memories but as real presences.

Dare to love and to be a real friend. The love you give and receive is a reality that will lead you closer and closer to God as well as to those whom God has given you to love.

—Henri J.M. Nouwen

18 | MAKE LOVE KNOWN!

Love is not loved, not known by his own creatures. O my Jesus! If I had a voice sufficiently loud and strong to be heard in every part of the world, I would cry out to make this Love known, loved, and honored by all men as the one immeasurable good.

—St. Mary Magdalene de Pazzi

19 | THE BENEFIT OF THE DOUBT

One of the chief differences between the saints and ourselves is that when things go wrong (and they never go absolutely right for very long), the saints take it for granted that God is treating them lovingly and wisely; we on the other hand, jump at once to the conclusion that God either does not mind what happens to us or is handing out a punishment. Sanctity always gives God the benefit of the doubt. In fact, it gives him the benefit of a certainty: He cannot go wrong; he has a plan; he never stops loving.

—*Dom Hubert van Zeller*

20 | LOVE MADE CREDIBLE

It is in them [the saints] that Christian love becomes credible; they are the poor sinners' guiding stars. But every one of them wishes to point completely away from himself and toward love.... The genuine saints desired nothing but the greater glory of God's love...

—*Hans Urs von Balthasar*

21 | MARRIED LOVE

It takes conversion to be able to love another, it takes deep conversion to love that person deeply. If husbands and wives understood this and put it into practice, divorces would vanish. And so would domestic fights and bickering and pouting and shouting disappear. Sympathetic listening to each other in differences of opinion would blossom. Each spouse would desire to do what the other prefers in practical matters…. Yes, christic love is a revolution.

—*Thomas Dubay, S.M.*

22 | **PERSPECTIVE**

Nothing makes us think more about ourselves than self-pity, danger or insecurity, so we can particularly relate thoughts of this kind to God's love. "I have a headache: Christ's head was crowned with thorns for the love of me. I dread the loss of my money or my job: Christ was stripped naked for the love of me. I am afraid of becoming helpless: for love of me Christ became a helpless infant. I am afraid of confined spaces: for love of me Christ was in the tomb. I dread my friends knowing that I am afraid: for love of me Christ sweated from fear. I am afraid to die: Christ died for love of me."

—*Caryll Houselander*

23 | THE FOUNTAIN OF LOVE

They [the lepers] asked the Lover which was the fountain of love. He answered that it was the one where the Beloved had cleansed us from our sins, and from which he gives us, as a free gift, that living water which brings whoever drinks it to eternal life in endless love.

—Rámon Lull

24 | WHY HE LOVES US

God does not love us because we are lovely or lovable; his love exists not on account of our character, but on account of his. Our highest experience is *responsive*, not initiative. And it is only because we are loved by him that we are lovable.

—Fulton J. Sheen

25 | UNCHANGING LOVE

Cross out the word "discouragement" from your dictionary of love; the more you feel your weakness and the difficulty of recollecting yourself, and the more hidden the Master seems, the more you must rejoice, for then you are giving to him...What does it matter what we feel; he is the Unchanging One.... He loves you today as he loved you yesterday and will love you tomorrow. I wish I could tell everyone what sources of strength, of peace and happiness they would find if only they would consent to live in this intimacy.

—*St. Elisabeth of the Trinity*

26 | TRUE FREEDOM

For Christians, love is a small word that relentlessly unpacks into a lot of other words: *truth*, *repentance*, *forgiveness*, *mercy*, *charity*, *courage*, *justice*. These are action words, all of them, including *truth*, because in accepting Jesus Christ, the Gospel says that we will know the truth and the truth will *make us free* (John 8:32)—not comfortable; not respected; but *free* in the real sense of the word: able to see and do what's right. This freedom is meant to be used in the service of others.

—*Archbishop Charles J. Chaput*

27 | GIFT OF LOVE

God's love is concrete...made up of words and gestures, which touches man in different situations, even in suffering and oppression, because it is love which frees and saves, which offers friendship and creates communion. All of this comes from the gift of the Spirit poured out as a gift of love into the hearts of believers to enable them to glorify God and announce his wonders to all peoples. Jesus Christ asks those who have been touched by the Father's love to love one another and to love everyone as he loved them.

—*Pope John Paul II*

28 | FORGET NOT LOVE

Pro amore, usque ad victimam (for love, for the sacrifice of my life).

—St. Maximilian Kolbe

29 | HOLD ON TO LOVE

Love was his meaning. Who showed it to you? Love. What did he show you? Love. Why did he show it? For love. Hold on to this and you will know and understand love more and more.... And so it was that I learned that love was our Lord's meaning. And I saw for certain, both here and elsewhere, that before he ever made us, God loved us; and that his love has never slackened, nor ever will. In this love all his works have been done, and in this love he has made everything serve us; and in this love our life is everlasting.

—Julian of Norwich

3o | PRACTICE MAKES PERFECT

The real love of man *must* depend on practice, and therefore, must begin by exercising itself on our friends around us, otherwise it will have no existence. By trying to love our relations and friends, by submitting to their wishes, though contrary to our own, by bearing with their infirmities, by overcoming their occasional waywardness by kindness, by dwelling on their excellences, and trying to copy them, thus it is that we form in our hearts that root of charity, which, though small at first, may, like the mustard seed, at last even overshadow the earth.

—*John Henry Newman*

31 | AN INFINITE RIVER

Because God is infinite his love is like sunlight. It does not divide. You cannot divide the sunlight itself. It is all the same. You can hide from it or stand in the shadows, but you do not affect the source of light itself…. The love of God is like an infinite river…. Like the Mississippi or the Hudson, it flows with an irresistible power, and its deep current is unhindered. You and I are in the river of God's love. If we swim with the tide, we will float along with that love. It will bring us where we are supposed to be.

—*Benedict J. Groeschel, C.F.R.*

32 | JOURNEYING TOWARD LOVE

You do not yet see God, but by loving your neighbor you gain the sight of God…. By loving your neighbor and being concerned about your neighbor, you make progress on your journey. Where is your journey if not to the Lord God, to him whom we must love with all our heart, and with all our soul and with all our mind? We have not reached the Lord, but we have our neighbors with us. So then, support him with whom you are traveling so that you may come to him with whom you long to dwell.

—St. Augustine

33 | TRANSFORMING LOVE

Love transforms one into what one loves.

—St. Catherine of Siena

34 | Love No Matter What

We must show constant, unconditional love and goodness to all, no matter how they treat us, because this is what God is like and does. He is forgiveness: a love always on tiptoe to forgive. As soon as we are there to receive he gives himself. We, too, must be like this, we must respond to others like this. Unless we do so we cannot receive God's love.

—Sr. Ruth Burrows, O.C.D.

35 | Our Vocation Is Love

The fundamental and innate vocation of every human is to love. The mutual love of a man and woman becomes an image of the absolute and unfailing love of God for man.

—Catechism of the Catholic Church, *1604*

36 | GOOD ADVICE

Love each other as God loves each one of you, with
an intense and particular love. Be kind to each other.
It is better to commit faults with gentleness than to
work miracles with unkindness.

—Mother Teresa of Calcutta

37 | LOVE THEM LIKE JESUS

Jesus crucified and forsaken is the way to love our
neighbor. His death on the cross, forsaken, is the
highest, divine, heroic lesson from Jesus about the
nature of love…. Give him your whole existence! Give
him your will…. His will is all this: Love God with
your whole heart! Love your neighbor as yourself.
Your neighbors…love them…and think that his or
her soul is worth the immense pain of Jesus forsaken.
Therefore, love them as if they *were* Jesus forsaken!

—Chiara Lubich

38 | **BE JOYFUL IN LOVING!**

Our love, the love which must reign in our hearts, must always be heavenly and joyous love. This is the way the Lord wants it.... Let us not offend this love by complaining or being gloomy.

—Chiara Lubich

39 | **THE REFLECTION OF LOVE**

I desire to love you, O my God, with a love that is patient, with a love that abandons itself wholly to you, with a love that acts, and most important of all, with a love that perseveres. Just as one who loves a creature thinks of it often, so let the lover of God have him often in his thoughts. The mirror into which we must look in order to attain divine love is Jesus Christ. If the actions of our neighbors had a hundred sides, we ought to look at them on the best side. When an

action is blameworthy, we should strive to see the good intentions behind it. Let us do everything for love and, remembering that love longs for love alone, nothing can appear hard to us.

—*St. Teresa Margaret Redi*

40 | LEARN TO LOVE

I have placed you in the midst of your fellows that you may do to them what you cannot do to me, that is to say, that you may love your neighbor freely without expecting any return from him, and what you do to him I count as done to me.

—The Dialogue *of St. Catherine of Siena*

41 | SEEING WITH THE EYES OF LOVE

I met the world and I found it no longer so wicked after all. Perhaps the things I had resented about the world when I left it were defects of my own that I had projected upon it. Now on the contrary, I found that everything stirred me with a deep and mute sense of compassion. Perhaps some of the people we saw going about the streets were hard and tough…but I did not stop to observe it because I seemed to have lost an eye for merely exterior detail and to have discovered, instead, a deep sense of respect and love and pity for the souls that such details never fully reveal. I went through the city, realizing for the first time in my life how good are all the people in the world and how much value they have in the sight of God.

—Thomas Merton

42 | THE HABIT OF CHARITY

Nothing deepens our mind as much as the habit of charity. Charity does not feed on surfaces. Its instinct is always to go deeper. Roots are its natural food. A man's surfaces are always worse than his real depths. There may be exceptions to this rule; but I believe them to be very rare...charity is the deepest view of life, and the nearest to God's view, and therefore also not merely the truest view, but the only view which is really true at all.

—Frederick Faber

43 | THE BOND OF LOVE

A lover's bonds are his wings. He is set free by entering into the bond of love. The arms of his beloved around him are as wide as the girdle around the world.... And as it is true with romantic love with its bonds of glorious liberty, so it is with all the other kinds of love—connubial love, maternal love, paternal love, filial love, and so forth: the bond that ties us to someone we love is a form of liberty to us. It is as strong as death, but is the very fountainhead of our life.

—Thomas Howard

44 | SIMPLY BECAUSE...

We are to love God above all things simply because God is. Our posture before God is always that of creature to creator, child to father, seeker to the one who satisfies all our most profound needs.

—Cardinal Donald Wuerl

45 | I WISH YOU GOOD

The Italians have a beautiful expression for love: *ti voglio bene*. Though commonly translated as "I love you," *ti voglio bene* more literally means "I wish you good" or "I want what is good for you." This phrase reminds us that love is not primarily about what good feelings may be stirring within. Even less about what I can get out of the relationship for myself. The fullness of love is looking outward toward my beloved and seeking what is best for that person, not just what is good for me.

—*Edward Sri*

46 | GOLDEN THREADS OF LOVE

Conjugal love, like romantic love, wants to be heroic; but it does not limit arbitrarily the scope of this heroism. In its desire to relate itself existentially to heroism, it will find it also in the modest deeds of everyday life, and will transform the tiresome routine of daily duties into golden threads binding oneself closer and closer to the beloved. There is in conjugal love a note of truth which is lacking in romantic love. It is a love that has been tested in the furnace of everyday trials and difficulties and has come out victoriously.... To be kind and loveable for a moment is no great feat. But to be loving day after day in the most varied and trying circumstances can be achieved only by one who truly loves.

—Alice von Hildebrand

47 | LOVING US RIGHT WHERE WE ARE

Christ's love for Peter was so boundless that in loving Peter he accomplished loving the person one sees. He did not say, "Peter must change first and become another man before I can love him again." No, just the opposite, he said, "Peter is Peter, and I love him; love, if anything will help him to become another man." ...Christian love grants the beloved all his imperfections and weaknesses and in all his changes remains with him, loving the person it sees.

—Søren Kierkegaard

48 | Suffering Love

O good Jesus, O sweetest Jesus, it was all to simply show us how much you love us. You spent yourself on our behalf. The grief, the tears, the spittle, the sneers, the cruelty and insults, the blows, the nails, the blood, all you suffered for us. And I weep.

—*St. Bonaventure*

49 | THE CONSOLATION OF LOVE IN DEATH

Real grief is not healed by time. If time does anything, it deepens our grief. The longer we live, the more fully we become aware of who she was for us, and the more intimately we experience what her love meant for us. Real, deep love is, as you know, very unobtrusive, seemingly easy and obvious, and so present that we take it for granted. Therefore, it is often only in retrospect—or better, in memory—that we fully realize its power and depth. Yes, indeed, love often makes itself visible in pain.

—Henri J.M. Nouwen, in a letter to his family
after his mother's death

50 | THE STARTING POINT OF LOVE

After many experiences and a lot of thinking, I am convinced that the objective starting point of love is the realization that I am needed by another. The person who objectively needs me the most is also, for me, objectively, the person I most need. This is a fragment of life's deep logic.

—Pope John Paul II

51 | HOLY LONGING

The whole of the good Christian is a holy longing. What you desire ardently, as yet you do not see…By withholding of the vision, God extends the longing; through longing he extends the soul, by extending it he makes room in it…let us long because we are to be filled…that is our life, to be exercised by the longing.

—St. Augustine

52 | SOURCE OF JOY

How many of us have not yet loved God? How many of us persist in refusing God's gift of himself?... We must fall down on our knees, and blind to our own preconceived ideas about God, recognize the Jesus whom we persecute. We must learn our catechism: that Jesus loves us, even though we have not yet shown our love for him; that he seeks us out, that he wants us to come to him, that he suffered and died for us...the power of love can also be a source of great joy. Only a word spoken to a loved one is sufficient to make him happy. To express our love for him, to try to please him, is to exercise a wonderful power which brings the beloved great joy and happiness.

—Louis Evely

53 | A Deeper Love in Marriage

Being in love is a good thing, but it is not the best thing. There are many things below it, but there are also things above it. You cannot make it the basis of a whole life. It is a noble feeling, but it is still a feeling.... Who could bear to live in that excitement for even five years?... But, of course, ceasing to be "in love" need not mean ceasing to love. Love in a second sense—love as distinct from "being in love" is not merely a feeling. It is deep unity, maintained by the will and deliberately strengthened by habit; reinforced by (in Christian marriages) the grace which both parents ask, and receive, from God. "Being in love" first moved them to promise fidelity; this quieter love enables them to keep the promise. It is on this love that the engine of marriage is run; being in love was the explosion that started it.

—*C.S. Lewis*

54 | **LOVE WILL CONQUER**

The Son is prepared, through Incarnation and redemption, to bring such a superabundance of love into the world that love will, in principle, outdo the power of sin.

—*Adrienne Von Speyer*

55 | **LOVE MADE MANIFEST**

The religion Jesus gave the world is an experience, not a body of ideas or principles. It is in being lived that it lives, as it is in loving that the love which it discloses at the heart of all creation becomes manifest.

—*Malcolm Muggeridge*

56 | GOD LOVES YOU, PERIOD

Dear Child of God, in our world it is often hard to remember that God loves you just as you are. God loves you not because you are good. No, God loves you, period. God loves us not because we are lovable. No, we are lovable precisely because God loves us. It is marvelous when you come to understand that you are accepted for who you are, apart from any achievement. It is liberating.

—Desmond Tutu

57 | LOVE'S SAFETY NET

If there be anywhere on earth a lover of God is always safe, I know nothing of it, for it was not shown to me. But this was shown: that in falling and rising again we are always kept in the same precious love.

—Julian of Norwich

58 | FINDING TRUE FRIENDSHIP

How precious our friendships are, and how near we are to each other when we are all one in Jesus!... So if you want to find your true friends, I will tell you where to look. Begin with God. He is the only source of true and eternal friendship.... He means everything to the kind of friends you seek. They talk of him and live for him and their whole lives are wrapped up in him.

—Francois Fénelon

59 | THE FATHER'S LOVING CARE

It has been said, "love is inventive." The fatherly heart of God is like a deep well that never runs dry. It forever brings up something different, some new thought for advising or helping His children who come to Him in their time of need…. And so we live with an excitement and a sense of expectation in our hearts, wondering in just what way the Father will meet our need *this* time…

—*Mother Basilia Schlink*

60 | A STAGGERING REALITY

It is staggering that God should love sinners; yet it is true. God loves creatures who have become unlovely and (one would have thought) unlovable. There was nothing whatever in the objects of his love to call it forth; nothing in us could attract or prompt it. Love among persons is awakened by something in the beloved, but the love of God is free, spontaneous, unevoked, uncaused. God loves people because he has chosen to love them...

—J.I. Packer

61 | ONLY ONE THING MATTERS

At the end of our life, we shall be judged by love.

—St. John of the Cross

62 | More Than Enough to Go Around

The heart of God is filled with inexhaustible love. Because it is infinite, everyone can possess it without lessening another's possession of it. God has enough love for the entire universe without being drained. When everything has been filled to the brim with God's love there remains an infinity of love in reserve.

—*St. Francis de Sales*

63 | The Way of Love

Ever since that memorable day, love seems to pierce me through and wrap me round, merciful love which makes a new creature of me, purifies my soul and leaves no trace of sin there…. Oh, what a comfort it is, this way of love! You may stumble on it, you may fail to correspond with grace given, but always love knows how to make the best of everything.

—*St. Thérèse of the Child Jesus*

64 | PURE LOVE

Pure love has no self-interest. Pure love does not gain strength through expectation, nor is it weakened by distrust. This is the love of the bride, for this is the bride—with all that means. Love is the being and the hope of a bride. She is full of it, and the bridegroom is contented with it. He asks nothing else, and she has nothing else to give. This is why he is the bridegroom and she is the bride; this love is the property only of the couple. No one else can share it, not even a son.

—St. Bernard of Clairvaux

65 | On Earth as It Is in Heaven

How good it is to love here on earth as they love in heaven and to learn to cherish one another in this world as we do eternally in the next! Here I do not refer to the simple love of charity we must have for all men but of that spiritual friendship by which two, three, or more souls share with one another their devotion and spiritual affections and establish a single spirit among themselves.

—St. Francis de Sales

66 | Love in Action

Love cannot remain by itself—it has no meaning. Love has to be put into action and that action is service. A mission of love can come only from union with God. From that union, love for the family, love for one's neighbor, love for the poor is the natural fruit.

—Mother Teresa of Calcutta

67 | A Child's Love

My God, you have done so much good for me, how can I not have for you the love of a child for her father. Put charity more strongly in my heart and preserve it there always, O my God.

—Sr. Marie de Mandat-Grancey

68 | Witnesses to Love

It was the Christian spirit of mutual love and communal charity which most impressed pagans. Tertullian quotes them as saying: "How these Christians love one another!"

—Paul Johnson

69 | STAIRWAY TO HEAVEN

Christ made love the stairway that would enable all Christians to climb to heaven. Hold fast to it, therefore, in all sincerity, give one another practical proof of it, and by your progress, make your ascent together.

—*St. Fulgence of Ruspe*

70 | GOD IN EVERYONE

We ought to respect the image of God in everyone. It is there.

—*St. Raphaela Mary*

71 | SURENESS OF HIS LOVE

One time...I was traveling, far from home and lonely, and I awoke in the night almost on the verge of weeping with a sense of futility, of being unloved and unwanted. And suddenly the thought came to me of my importance as a daughter of God, daughter of a King, and I felt a sureness of God's love and at the same time a conviction that one of the greatest injustices (if one can put it that way) which one can do to God is to distrust his love, not realize his love.

—*Dorothy Day*

72 | THE BIRTH OF FRIENDSHIP

Friendship arises out of mere companionship when two or more of the companions discover that they have in common some insight of interest or even taste which others do not share and which, till that moment, each believed to be his own unique treasure (or burden). The typical expression of opening friendship would be something like, "What? You too? I thought I was the only one." It is when two such persons discover one another, when, whether with immense difficulties and semi-articulate fumblings or with what would seem to us amazing and elliptical speed, they share their vision—it is then that Friendship is born.

—*C.S. Lewis*

73 | FAITHFUL LOVE

Love him, therefore and hold him for your friend, for, when all others forsake you, he will not forsake you, or suffer you finally to perish.... Commit yourself to his fidelity, and he will be with you and help you when all others forsake you. Your Beloved is of such nature that he will not admit any other love, for he alone will have the love of your heart...

—Thomas à Kempis

74 | FIRE OF LOVE

And yet, God is all love. This gentle Savior pleads with us from the Host: "Love Me as I have loved you; abide in My love! I came to cast the fire of my love on the earth, and My most ardent desire is that it should set your hearts on fire."

—St. Peter Julian Eymard

75 | LOVE IS IN THE DETAILS

What can a person do who tries to love God tremendously? Everything, from putting the lights off, to refraining from changing clothes every five minutes, to being indifferent to food, to going where God calls you. Once I know God's will I am going to try to do it perfectly. My heart swells and I say, "This also, Lord, for love of you."... It never occurs to me that I can possibly separate anything from love. Wherever you go you will certainly have to do little things. Try to do them without love, and see what happens. But doing little things with our whole hearts is our vocation.

—*Catherine de Hueck Doherty*

76 | A WONDERFUL ADVENTURE

I conceived a dream: to offer you my whole life, the only life I have to live, for an eternal and unalterable ideal.

I have decided! If I fulfill your will you will achieve this ideal in me, and I will throw myself into this wonderful adventure.

I have chosen you, I have no regrets.

I hear you say to me: "Remain in me. Remain in my love!"

But how can I remain in another?

Only love can achieve this extraordinary mystery.

I understand that you want my whole life.

"Everything! And for your love!"

—Cardinal Francis Xavier Nguyen Van Thuan

77 | GOD IS PRESENT

In true love it is not we who love the afflicted in God;
it is God in us who loves them.... Compassion and
gratitude come down from God, and when they are
exchanged in a glance, God is present at the point
where the edges of those who give and those who
receive meet.

—Simone Weil

78 | A FAITHFUL FRIEND

Friendship has to be constant and persevering in its affections: we do not change friends as children do, for they allow themselves to be carried away by the free and easy wave of feelings. Open your heart to your friend, so that he be faithful and so that he is united to the joy of life. A faithful friend, really, is life-saving medicine, an elixir of life... Do not abandon him at the moment of need. Do not forget about him. Do not deny him your affection. For friendship is the support of life. We carry one another's burdens...

—St. Ambrose of Milan

79 | NOTHING ELSE

What I seek is love. I want nothing else but to love you, O Jesus.

—St. Thérèse of the Child Jesus

80 | LOVE ALWAYS OBEYS

...To share my bread down to the last bite with any pauper, any stranger who appears, receiving every human being like a beloved brother. My ordinary inclination is for solitude, stability, silence. But if I believe I am called to something other, I obey. Love always obeys when it has God as its object.

—*Charles de Foucauld*

81 | IT IS GOOD THERE IS A YOU

Love, says Augustine, means first of all: I am glad that you exist! It is good that there is a "you"! Love begins with goodwill, and from this it then follows that I also do good to the other person.... Am I good to my neighbor? Not just the question of whether I like him. And here we understand why Jesus insepa-rably ties together the love of God and neighbor.... When I take into consideration that God totally loves this neighbor who is so troublesome to me and that he accepts even me with all my faults and says Yes to me, then surely I can try to love my neighbor as well.

—*Cardinal Christoph Schönborn*

82 | I LOVE YOU ANYWAY

I am so fickle, so forgetful. In my self-will I walk my own way. How often I am carried off on a tangent—away from my fundamental desire to love my Lord! Even so, when I listen with all my heart, I can hear my Father say: "I love you anyway. I love you with an age-old love, and it will never change because I am God and not man." Thank you for loving me, Lord, and I love you too!

—*David E. Rosage*

83 | UNFATHOMABLE TRUTH

It is difficult for me to fathom this truth: that God first loved me. I must keep reminding myself that I would not be enjoying my gifted life if he had not loved me before I could even respond to his love. Somehow I feel I must earn God's love, I must merit it. But that is impossible. All that God asks of me is to let him love me just as I am. It is only when I experience his love for me that I am able to respond in love to him, and to others.

—David E. Rosage

84 | AWAITED BY LOVE

She came to know that this Lord even knew her, that he had created her—that he actually loved her. She too was loved, and by none other than the supreme "Paron," before whom all other masters are themselves no more than lowly servants. She was known and loved and she was awaited.... Now she had "hope"—no longer simply the modest hope of finding masters who would be less cruel, but the great hope: "I am definitely loved and whatever happens to me—I am awaited by this Love. And so my life is good."

—*Pope Benedict XVI and St. Josephine Bakhita*

85 | THE MEASURE OF LOVE

Marriage based on exclusive and definitive love becomes the icon of the relationship between God and his people and vice versa. God's way of loving becomes the measure of human love.

—*Pope Benedict XVI*

86 | No Go-Between

Our Lord sends neither angels nor ministers to assure us of his love; he comes in person. Love will have no go-between. And so he perpetuates himself only to tell us over and over again: "I love you. You see that I love you!" Our Lord was so afraid we might forget him that he took up his abode among us. He made his home with us so that we might not be able to think of him without thinking of his love.... Whoever gives serious thought to the Eucharist and especially whoever partakes of it, cannot help feeling that our Lord loves him. He feels that he is loved as a child and that he has a right to come to his Father and speak to him.... Such is the personal love of Jesus for us.

—*St. Peter Julian Eymard*

8₇ | THE POWER OF GRACE

O God, one in the Holy Trinity, I want to love you as no human soul has ever loved you before; and although I am utterly miserable and small, I have, nevertheless, cast the anchor of my trust deep down into the abyss of Your mercy.... Let no soul, even the most miserable, fall prey to doubt; for as long as one is alive, each one can become a great saint, so great is the power of God's grace.

—St. Faustina Kowalska

88 | Now Is the Time to Love

A woman who really does love does not say to herself: "Tomorrow, I will love my husband, tomorrow, I will love my children, tomorrow, I will have time to think of them." But it is now that she loves them, because each task is performed in anticipation of their return. Now is the time that she loves them and she totally commits herself in everything she does.

That is exactly what we must do. There is no question of us waiting...it is now, here...that God is waiting for you. There lies your eternity, your infinite communion, because each human act, if it is a gift of ourselves, is an act of creating eternity.

—Fr. Maurice Zundel

89 | **LOVE MARY**

Do not fear loving Our Lady too much for you will never come to love her as Jesus loved her.

—St. Maximilian Kolbe

90 | **INFINITE VALUE**

And God has given me the understanding that there is but one thing that is of infinite value in his eyes, and that is love of God; love, love and once again, love; and nothing can compare with a single act of pure love of God.

—St. Faustina Kowalska

91 | LOVE IS ACTION

Charity, a supernatural virtue, is rarely considered as such, even by Christians. It is life, love, action; let us guard against practicing it in a manner that is sluggish, passive, lifeless.

—Elizabeth Leseur

92 | SONG OF LOVE

Let us love. Let our souls and our lives be a perpetual song of love for God first of all and for all human beings who suffer, love, and mourn.

—Elizabeth Leseur

93 | LOVING FATHER

Oh, open your heart to the Father, the most loving of all fathers, and let him act freely within you. Let us not be stingy with One who enriches us even too much, whose generosity is endless and knows no limits. Your only thought should be to love God and to grow more and more in virtue and in holy love, which is the bond of Christian perfection. The Lord is a Father, the most tender and best of fathers. The Lord is with you, not as a judge but as a loving Father, a beloved Spouse. He is with you—patient, suffering, eager—when you are crushed, trampled upon, heartbroken, in the shadows of the night, and even more so in the desolation of Gethsemane.

—*St. Padre Pio*

94 | THE SUPREME TESTIMONY OF LOVE

Since Jesus, the Son of God, manifested his charity by laying down his life for us, no one has greater love than he who lays down his life for Christ and his brothers. From the earliest times, then, some Christians have been called upon—and some will always be called upon—to give this supreme testimony of love to all men, but especially to persecutors. The Church, therefore, considers martyrdom as an exceptional gift and as the highest proof of love. Though few are presented with such an opportunity, nevertheless, all must be prepared to confess Christ before men, and to follow him along the way of the cross through persecutions which the Church will never fail to suffer.

—Dogmatic Constitution on the Church, 42

95 | IT WILL DECIDE EVERYTHING

Nothing is more practical than finding God, that is, than falling in love in a quite absolute, final way. What you are in love with, what seizes your imagination, will affect everything. It will decide what will get you out of bed in the morning, what you will do with your evenings, how you will spend your weekends, what you read, who you know, what breaks your heart, and what amazes you with joy and gratitude. Fall in love, stay in love, and it will decide everything.

—Fr. Pedro Arrupe, S.J.

96 | THE ICON OF CHRIST

The hunger for God can only be satisfied by a love that is face to face, person to person. It is only in the eyes of another that we can find the Icon of Christ. We must make the other person aware we love him. If we do, he will know that God loves him. He will never hunger again.

—Catherine de Hueck Doherty

97 | LOVE FOR A LIFETIME

There are people who try to ridicule, or even to deny, the idea of a faithful bond which lasts a lifetime. These people—you can be very sure—do not know what love is.

—Pope John Paul II

98 | THEY DID IT FOR LOVE

The saints have never attached importance to what their hands did; they did what they had to do but they did it for love.

—Fr. Père Jacques Bunel

99 | HOW MUCH?

The measure of love is to love without measure.

—St. Francis de Sales

100 | MY ONLY DESIRE

I love you, O my God, and my only desire is to love you until the last breath of my life. I love you, O my infinitely lovable God, and I would rather die loving you, than live without loving you. I love you, Lord, and the only grace I ask is to love you eternally.... My God, if my tongue cannot say in every moment that I love you, I want my heart to repeat it to you as often as I draw breath.

—*St. John Marie Vianney*

101 | WOOED BY LOVE

As God sees the world tottering to ruin because of fear, he acts unceasingly to bring it back by love, to invite it by grace, to hold it by charity and clasp it firmly with affection.

—*St. Peter Chrysologus*

102 | PERSEVERANCE

I desire to love you, O my God, with a love that is patient, with a love that abandons itself wholly to you, with a love that acts, and most important of all, with a love that perseveres.

—*St. Teresa Margaret Redi*

103 | IRONY

I have found the paradox, that if you love until it hurts, there can be no more hurt, only more love.

—*Mother Teresa of Calcutta*

104 | IRRESISTIBLE LOVE

The Good is undying and the victory must remain with God, even if it sometimes seems useless for us to spread love in the world. Nevertheless, one sees again and again that the human heart is attuned to love, and it cannot withstand its power in the long run, if it is truly based on God and not on creatures. We want to continue to do and offer everything so that love and peace may soon reign again.

—Fr. Engelmar Unzeitig

105 | PUT LOVE IN

Where there is no love, put love, and you will draw love out.

—St. John of the Cross

106 | OVERWHELMING LOVE

The love of God makes light of apparent obstacles or barriers. Give him your trust, your confidence. One day you will thank God, in heaven, for the prayers he has answered here on earth, not in your way, but in his. One day you will thank God for having loved you in the way God does love, with all the height, all the breadth, all the depth of a love which passes human understanding and overwhelms us. Then, the whole of eternity will not be too long for us to say, "thank you."

—*Cardinal Leon Joseph Suenens*

107 | SCHOOL OF LOVE

We are put on earth for a little space, that we may learn to bear the beams of love.

—William Blake

108 | HEALING LOVE

It is not on our forgiveness any more than on our goodness that the world's healing hinges. But on His. When He tells us to love our enemies, He gives, along with the command, the love itself.

—Corrie Ten Boom

109 | LOVE ME IN THEM

I [God] ask you to love me with the same love with which I love you. But for me you cannot do this, for I loved you without being loved. Whatever love you have for me you owe me, so you love me not gratuitously but out of duty, while I love you not out of duty but gratuitously. So you cannot give me the kind of love I ask of you. That is why I have put you among your neighbors: so that you can do for them what you cannot do for me—that is, love them without any concern for thanks and without looking for any profit yourself. And whatever you do for them I will consider done for me.

—*St. Catherine of Siena*

110 | **THE NATURE OF LOVE**

Love wants joint ownership of property. It wants to share fortune and misfortune. It is in the nature of love—its instinct to give everything with joy and happiness.

—*St. Katharine Drexel*

111 | **HUMAN VALUES**

Let us never be afraid to remind the world that standing above purely economic, material, or psychological values, there are human values, values of the heart, moral and spiritual values, values that find their source and their strength in the intimacy of a united family where peace and love reign supreme.

—*Georges Vanier*

112 | IDOLATRY

Thus does the world forget you, its Creator, and falls in love with what you have created instead of You.

—St. Augustine of Hippo

113 | CREATIVE LOVE

God is he who sees, but his seeing is an act of love. With his seeing, he embraces his creatures, affirms them, and encourages them, since he hates nothing that he has created…. The love of God is creative and redemptive. It created the world out of nothing and re-created the world after it had fallen. His seeing is not the kind that merely looks at something: it is creative love; it is the power that enables things to be themselves and rescues them from degeneration and

decay. God turns his face to man and thereby gives himself to man. By looking at me he enables me to be myself. The soul lives on the loving gaze of God: this is an infinitely deep and blessed mystery.

—Romano Guardini

114 | LESSONS IN LOVE

You may not be in love with God, but God is most certainly in love with you. Always remember that. He has given you two tutors who will give you your first lessons in mature religious response. They are called love and pain. It is love which will attach you to God, and pain will detach you from exclusive entanglement with the goods of this world.

—Cardinal Basil Hume

115 | NOTHING IS SWEETER

Nothing, therefore, is sweeter than love, nothing higher, nothing stronger, nothing larger, nothing more joyful, nothing fuller, and nothing better in heaven nor in earth; for love descends from God and may not rest finally in anything lower than God.

—Thomas à Kempis

116 | **THY WILL BE DONE**

Do you think it's some small matter to have a friend
[Christ] like this at your side?... [As we begin to grow
in union with God] he begins to commune with the
soul in so intimate a friendship that he not only gives
it back its own will but gives it his.

—*St. Teresa of Avila*

117 | **LITTLE KNOWN, LITTLE LOVED**

Is it possible for man to love that which he does not
know? Can he love ardently that which he knows but
imperfectly? Why then is the adorable Jesus, Eternal
and Incarnate Wisdom, loved so little? Because he is
not known, or known but little.

—*St. Louis-Marie de Montfort*

118 | REMEMBER TRUTH

We see difficulties in the lives of our children, our spouse, our friends, our relatives. We say, "Why did this have to happen?" It takes faith to be able to say, "My God is in charge, and my God is a God of love." But that is what we need to say. That is the truth that we must proclaim to ourselves over and over. "God I'm going to remember that you are a God of faithful love. I'm not going to harden my heart because of what has happened. I'm not going to close myself off from you. I'm going to remind myself that you love me and that you will never leave me. I'm going to put my faith in that fact and trust you to reveal your love and care to me in due time." After all, that is what Jesus did in the crisis of his life: he trusted in God's faithful love for him.

—Sr. Ann Shields, S.G.L.

119 | **LOVE YOUR ENEMIES**

Asked if she forgave her murderer, she replied, "Yes, for the love of Jesus I forgive him…and I want him to be with me in Paradise."

—Pope Pius XII, speaking about St. Maria Goretti
before her death

120 | **ONE GOAL**

Everything comes from love, all is ordained for the salvation of man; God does nothing without this goal in mind.

—St. Catherine of Siena

The Voices

St. Agnes (c. 291–c. 304) was only thirteen years old when she suffered martyrdom for her faith. She is the patron saint of chastity, rape victims, and virgins.

Mother Mary Angelica of the Annunciation (1923–) is an American Franciscan nun best known as a television personality and the founder of the Eternal Word Television Network in Irondale, Alabama.

St. Ambrose of Milan (c. 330–397) was an archbishop of Milan who became one of the most influential ecclesiastical figures of the fourth century. He was one of the four original doctors of the Church.

St. Thomas Aquinas (c. 1225–1274) was a Dominican priest and one of the greatest theologians of all time. He is called the Angelic Doctor of the Church.

Pedro Arrupe, S.J., (1907–1991) was the twenty-eighth superior general of the Society of Jesus. He was a man of great spiritual depth who was committed to justice.

St. Augustine of Hippo (354–430) was a bishop in North Africa, a prolific writer, and a Doctor of the Church.

Pope Benedict XVI (1927–) began his pontificate in 2005. He is a scholar of the liturgy and previously served as the Vatican's chief doctrinal official.

St. Bernard of Clairvaux (1090–1153) was a Cistercian abbot, mystic, spiritual writer, and Doctor of the Church.

Cardinal Joseph Bernardin (1928–1996) served as Archbishop of Chicago from 1982 until his death. In 1996, Bernardin was awarded the Presidential Medal of Freedom, the highest civilian honor bestowed on individuals who have made significant contributions to their communities and the nation.

William Blake (1757–1827) was an English poet, painter, and printmaker. Largely unrecognized during his lifetime, Blake is now considered a seminal figure in both the poetry and visual arts of the Romantic Age.

St. Bonaventure (1221–1274) was an Italian medieval scholastic theologian and philosopher.

Père Jacques Bunel de Jésus (1900–1945) was a Carmelite priest and headmaster of the Petit Collège Sainte-Thérèse de l' Enfant-Jésus. He was named one of the "Righteous Among the Nations" by Israel in 1985, as a non-Jew who risked his life during the Holocaust to save Jews.

Sister Ruth Burrows, a Carmelite nun, lives in Norfolk, England, and is the author of three outstanding books on prayer.

St. Catherine of Siena (1347–1380) was a philosopher, theologian, and Doctor of the Church. She worked to bring the papacy of Gregory XI back to Rome from its displacement in France, and to establish peace among the Italian city-states. Along with St. Francis of Assisi, she is one of the two patron saints of Italy.

Charles J. Chaput (1944–) is the current Archbishop of Philadelphia and the first Native American archbishop.

Servant of God Dorothy Day (1897–1980) was an American journalist, social activist, and devout Catholic convert. In the 1930s, Day helped establish the Catholic Worker movement.

Catherine de Hueck Doherty (1896–1985) was a pioneer of social justice and foundress of the Madonna House Apostolate. She was also a prolific writer and a dedicated wife and mother.

St. Katharine Drexel (1858–1955) was born into a wealthy family in Philadelphia and devoted her life to the poor. She was the founder of Xavier University in New Orleans, the first Catholic university in the United States for African Americans.

St. Francis de Sales (1567–1622) was a bishop of Geneva and leader of the Catholic Reformation. His book *Introduction to the Devout Life* became a classic spiritual guide for living an authentic Christian life.

St. Elisabeth of the Trinity (1880–1906) was a French Carmelite nun and religious writer who died at age twenty-six, only five years after entering the convent. Although she suffered greatly, she lived with gratitude and love of the Trinity.

St. Josemaría Escrivá (1902–1975), the founder of Opus Dei, was canonized by Pope John Paul II, who declared him as "counted among the great witnesses of Christianity."

Louis Evely (1910–1985) was a Christian spiritual writer from Belgium.

Frederick Faber (1814–1863) was a noted English hymn writer and theologian, who converted from Anglicanism to Catholicism and became a priest.

Francois de Salignac de La Mothe Fénelon (1651–1715) was a French bishop, theologian, and author.

Blessed Charles de Foucauld (1858–1916) was a French Catholic religious and priest living among the Tuareg in the Sahara in Algeria. He was assassinated in 1916 is considered to be a martyr. His inspiration and writings led to the founding of the Little Brothers of Jesus.

St. Fulgence of Ruspe (c. 462–c. 533) was born into a noble family of Carthage, became a bishop in North Africa in the fifth and sixth century, and was canonized as a Christian saint.

Pope St. Gregory the Great (540–604) was known for his zeal, and in spite of his many bodily sufferings, he is remembered for his magnificent contributions to the Liturgy of the Mass and Office.

Fr. Benedict J. Groeschel, C.F.R. (1933–) is a retreat master, psychologist, well-known author, and one of the founders of the Franciscan Friars of the Renewal.

Romano Guardini (1885–1968) was a Catholic priest, author, and academic. He was one of the most important figures in Catholic intellectual life in the twentieth century.

Caryll Houselander (1901–1954) was an artist and prolific author who enjoyed enormous literary success in the 1940s and 1950s.

Thomas Howard is a highly acclaimed writer and scholar, raised in a prominent Evangelical home (his sister is well-known author and former missionary Elisabeth Elliot). He entered the Catholic Church in 1985.

Cardinal George Basil Hume, O.S.B. (1923–1999) was a monk for nearly sixty years before his appointment as Archbishop of Westminster.

St. John of the Cross (1542–1591) was a Spanish Carmelite reformer, mystical writer, and Doctor of the Church.

Pope John Paul II (1920–2005) reigned as pope for almost twenty-seven years and played a key role in the fall of communism. He is one of the most beloved popes of the modern era.

Paul Johnson (1928–) is an English journalist, historian, speechwriter, and author.

Julian of Norwich (1342–1423), a hermit and one of the greatest English mystics, wrote about God's merciful love and compassion.

Thomas à Kempis (c. 1380–1471) was a late medieval Catholic monk and the probable author of *The Imitation of Christ*, which is one of the best known Christian books on devotion.

Søren Kierkegaard (1813–1855) was a profound and prolific writer in the Danish "golden age" of intellectual and artistic activity.

St. Maximilian Kolbe (1894–1941) was a Polish Franciscan priest and founder of the Knights of Mary Immaculate. His martyrdom in Auschwitz was said to be "like a powerful shaft of light in the darkness of the camp."

St. Faustina Kowalska (1905–1938) was a Polish nun and mystic who, after receiving visions of Jesus, introduced the popular devotion to Divine Mercy.

Peter Kreeft, Ph.D. (1939–) a convert to Catholicism, is a professor of philosophy at Boston College and a well-known author and speaker.

Elizabeth Leseur (1866–1914) lived a life of simplicity amidst the swirl of Parisian society, using her serious illness and her husband's constant efforts to destroy her faith as means to grow in love for him and for God.

Clive Staples Lewis (1898–1963) was an Irish-born British novelist, academic, theologian, and Christian apologist. He is also known for his fiction, especially *The Screwtape Letters* and *The Chronicles of Narnia*.

Sister Marie de Mandat-Grancey (1837–1915) was a member of the daughters of charity of St. Vincent De Paul in Paris. She is best known for her involvement in the discovery of the House of the Virgin Mary in Ephesus, Turkey.

Erasmo Leiva-Merikakas, now Brother Simeon, is a Cistercian monk and the author of *Fire of Mercy: Heart of the Word*, a three-volume commentary on St. Matthew's Gospel.

Chiara Lubich (1920–2008) was an Italian Catholic activist and leader and the foundress of the Focolare Movement.

Ramón Lull (c. 1232–c. 1315) was a Majorcan writer and philosopher, logician, and a Franciscan tertiary.

Thomas Merton (1915–1968) was a Catholic writer, social activist, and Trappist monk of the Abbey of Gethsemani, Kentucky.

St. Louis-Marie de Montfort (1673–1716) was a French Roman Catholic priest and confessor. He was known in his time as a preacher and for his particular devotion to the Blessed Virgin Mary and the practice of consistently praying the rosary.

St. Thomas More (1478–1535) a lawyer, scholar, author, and Lord Chancellor of England was martyred for his faith and is known for his courage and fortitude in the face of death.

Malcolm Muggeridge (1903–1990) was a British journalist, social critic, and author. An avowed atheist, he moved gradually to embrace Roman Catholicism at age seventy-nine.

Cardinal John Henry Newman (1801–1890) was a prolific English author who converted from Anglicanism to Catholicism and became an Oratorian priest and cardinal.

Henri Nouwen (1932–1996) was a Dutch-born Catholic priest and writer who taught at influential universities for almost two decades until he left to join Daybreak L'Arche community in Canada, living and working with the mentally handicapped until his death.

J.I. Packer (1926–) is a Christian theologian in the Anglican and Reformed traditions. He currently serves as the Board of Governors' Professor of Theology at Regent College in Vancouver, British Columbia. He is considered one of the most influential evangelicals in North America.

St. Mary Magdalene de Pazzi (1566–1607) was an Italian Carmelite mystic whose life was characterized by an early love of prayer and penance, charity for the poor, and an evangelical spirit.

St. Padre Pio of Pietrelcina (1887–1968) was a Capuchin priest and mystic who bore the wounds of Christ in his body.

Pope Pius XII (1876–1958) reigned as pope from 1939 until his death.

St. Raphaela Mary (1850–1925) founded the Institute of Handmaids of the Sacred Heart of Jesus, which the spirituality of St. Ignatius of Loyola, a community that spread quickly throughout Spain.

St. Teresa Margaret Redi (1747–1770) was driven by the desire to "return love for love." She entered the Carmelite convent in Florence at the age of seventeen, advanced rapidly in holiness, and died an extraordinary death at twenty-two.

Monsignor David E. Rosage (1913–2009) was a prolific writer and the founder and director of Immaculate Heart Retreat Center in the diocese of Spokane, Washington.

Mother Basilea Schlink (1904–2001) founded the Evangelical Sisterhood of Mary in post-war Germany. She wrote prolifically about how to walk the pathway of the cross with joy.

Cardinal Christoph Schönborn (1945–), the Archbishop of Vienna, Austria, is a highly regarded author and the coeditor of the *Catechism of the Catholic Church*.

St. Elizabeth Ann Seton (1774–1821), the first native-born citizen of the United States to be canonized by the Roman Catholic Church, was a wife, mother, and founder of the Sisters of Charity. She is popularly considered a patron saint of Catholic schools.

Fulton J. Sheen (1895–1979) was an American archbishop and author known for his preaching and especially for his work on television and radio.

Sr. Ann Shields, S.G.L., is a member of the Servants of God's Love, a religious community in Ann Arbor, Michigan. She is an internationally noted speaker, author, and host of the daily radio program *Food for the Journey*.

Adrienne Von Speyer (1902–1967) was a Swiss medical doctor and the author of over sixty books on spirituality and theology.

Edward Sri is a nationally known Catholic speaker and the author of several bestselling books. He is provost and professor of theology and Scripture at the Augustine Institute and founding leader with Curtis Martin of FOCUS.

Cardinal Leon Joseph Suenens (1904–1996), served as Archbishop of Mechelen-Brussel from 1961 to 1979, and was elevated to the cardinalate in 1962. He was a leading voice at the Second Vatican Council.

Corrie Ten Boom (1892–1983) was a Dutch Christian, who with her father and other family members helped many Jews escape the Nazi Holocaust during World War II. Her family was arrested due to an informant, and Corrie and her sister Betsie were sent to the Ravensbruck concentration camp, where only Corrie survived.

St. Teresa of Avila (1515-1582) was a prominent Spanish mystic, Carmelite nun, writer of the Counter Reformation, and Doctor of the Church. She was a reformer of the Carmelite Order and—along with John of the Cross—founded the Discalced Carmelites.

Mother Teresa of Calcutta (1910–1997) was an Albanian Catholic nun with Indian citizenship who founded the Missionaries of Charity in Calcutta, India, in 1950 and won the Nobel Peace Prize in 1979.

St. Thérèse of the Child Jesus (1873–1897), also known as Thérèse of Lisieux, was a French Carmelite nun, mystic, and Doctor of the Church. One of the most popular saints of the twentieth century, she was canonized less than thirty years after her death at the age of twenty-four and is best known for her "Little Way" of holiness.

Cardinal Francis Xavier Nguyen Van Thuan (1928–2002) was taken to North Vietnam in 1975 where, without being tried or sentenced, he was imprisoned for more than thirteen years, nine of which were spent in solitary confinement. In 1991 he was exiled from Vietnam, never to return to his homeland. He always lived and preached forgiveness and reconciliation.

Desmond Tutu (1931–) is a South African civil rights activist and retired Anglican bishop who rose to worldwide fame during the 1980s as an opponent of apartheid. He was the first black South African Archbishop of Cape Town.

Fr. Engelmar Unzeitig (1911–1945) has been called the "Angel of Dachau." He studied Russian in order to be able to help the prisoners from Eastern Europe. In 1944 he volunteered to help in the typhoid barrack where he contracted the disease himself and died.

Georges Vanier (1888–1967) was a war hero and diplomat who served as Governor General of Canada. He rarely made any major decision without first considering its implications in prayer. His biographer noted that "he was a man who walked with God."

Dom Hubert Van Zeller, O.S.B. (1905–1984), a Benedictine monk in England, was a sculptor and author of over fifty books on the spiritual life.

St. John Marie Vianney (1786–1859) served humbly as a priest in rural French parishes. He is the patron saint of all priests and is often referred to as the "Curé d'Ars."

Hans Urs von Balthasar (1905–1988) was a Swiss theologian and priest. He is considered one of the most important theologians of the twentieth century.

Alice von Hildebrand (1923–) is a Catholic philosopher, theologian, former professor, author, and lecturer. She was married to the famous philosopher and theologian Dietrich von Hildebrand.

Simone Weil (1909–1943) was a French philosopher, mystic, and social activist.

Cardinal Donald Wuerl (1940–) is the current archbishop of Washington, D.C.

Fr. Maurice Zundel (1897–1975) was a Swiss theologian.

The Sources

1. Fulton Sheen, *From the Angel's Blackboard* (Liguori, Mo.: Triumph, 1995), p. 206.

2. C.S. Lewis, *The Four Loves* (New York, N.Y.: Houghton Mifflin Harcourt, 1991), p. 121.

3. Thérèse of Lisieux, quoted in Cindy Cavnar, ed., *Prayers and Meditations of Thérèse of Lisieux* (Ann Arbor, Mich.: Servant, 1992), p. 61.

4. Mother Teresa of Calcutta, quoted in C.A. Devolld, ed., *In Defense of the Faithful: The Scriptural Truth of Catholicism* (n.p.: iUniverse, 2006), p. 63.

5. John of the Cross, quoted in *Ascent to Love, The Spiritual Teaching of St. John of the Cross*, Ruth Burrows (Denville, N.J.: Dimension, 1987), p. 19.

6. Thérèse of the Child Jesus, quoted in Cavnar, p. 62.

7. Cardinal Joseph Bernardin, *The Journey to Peace, Reflections on Faith, Embracing Suffering, and Finding New Life* (New York: Doubleday, 2001), p. 67.

8. Mother Angelica, quoted in Raymond Arroyo, ed., *Mother Angelica's Little Book of Life Lessons and Everyday Spirituality* (New York: Doubleday, 2007), p. 20.

9. Josemaria Escrivá, *The Way* (London: Scepter, 1982), p. 143.

10. Josemaria Escrivá, *The Way*, p. 143.

11. Gregory the Great, quoted in Jill Haak Adels, ed., *The Wisdom of the Saints: An Anthology* (Oxford, U.K.: Oxford University Press, 1989), p. 40.

12. Catherine de Hueck Doherty, *The Gospel without Compromise* (Combermere, Ontario: Madonna House, 1989), p. 77.

13. John Paul II, *Lessons for Living*, Joseph Durepos, ed. (Chicago: Loyola, 2004), p. 94.

14. Peter Kreeft, *Before I Go, Letters to Our Children about What Really Matters* (Lanham, Md.: Sheed & Ward, 2007), p. 11.

15. Erasmo Leiva-Merikakas, *The Way of the Disciple* (San Francisco: Ignatius, 2003), p. 96.

16. Bernard of Clairvaux, quoted in Rahul Sharma, ed., *Of Head and Heart* (St. Paul, Minn.: Paragon, 2012), p. 52.

17. Henri J.M. Nouwen, *The Inner Voice of Love* (New York: Image Doubleday), pp. 80–81.

18. Mary Magdalene de Pazzi, quoted in Rhonda De Sola Chervin, ed., *Quotable Saints* (Ann Arbor, Mich.: Servant, 1992), p. 130.

19. Dom Hubert Van Zeller, *Holiness, a Guide for Beginners* (Manchester, N.H.: Sophia Institute, 1997), p. 48.

20. Hans Urs Von Balthasar, *Love Alone is Credible* (San Francisco: Ignatius, 2004), pp. 120–121.

21. Thomas Dubay, S.M, *Deep Conversion, Deep Prayer* (San Francisco: Ignatius, 2006), p. 71.

22. Caryll Houselander, *A Rocking-Horse Catholic* (New York: Sheed and Ward, 1955), p. 67.

23. Ramón Lull, quoted in Francis Fernandez, *In Conversation with God* (London: Scepter, 2010), p. 98.

24. Fulton J. Sheen, *From the Angel's Blackboard*, p. 99.

25. Elisabeth of the Trinity, quoted in Ruth Burrows, O.C.D., *The Essence of Prayer* (London: Burns & Oates, 2006), pp. 135–136.

26. Charles J. Chaput, *Render unto Caesar* (New York: Random House, 2009), p. 38.

27. John Paul II, *Rising in Christ: Meditations of Living the Resurrection* (Ijamsville, Md.: The Word Among Us, 2005), p. 174.

28. Maximilian Kolbe, quoted in Andre Frossard, *Forget Not Love, The Passion of Maximilian Kolbe*, (San Francisco: Ignatius, 1991), p. 46.

29. Julian of Norwich, *Revelations of Divine Love*, Clifton Wolters, trans. (London: Penguin, 1966), pp. 211–212.

30. John Henry Newman, *The Heart of Newman*, Erich Prsywara, S.J., ed. (San Francisco: Ignatius, 1997), p. 266.

31. Benedict J. Groeschel, C.F.R., *Stumbling Blocks or Stepping Stones, Spiritual Answers to Psychological Questions* (New York: Paulist, 1987), pp. 114–115.

32. Augustine of Hippo, quoted in Joseph Durepos, ed., *The Grandeur of God*, (Chicago: Loyola, 2005), pp. 12–13.

33. *Catherine of Siena: The Dialogue* (New York: Paulist, 1980), pp. 115–116.

34. Ruth Burrows, O.C.D., *The Essence of Prayer* (London: Burns & Oates, 2006), p. 23.

35. *The Catechism of the Catholic Church* (Washington, D.C.: USCCB, 1994), p. 401.

36. Mother Teresa of Calcutta, quoted in Durepos, p. 135.

37. Chiara Lubich, *Jesus, the Heart of His Message* (Hyde Park, N.Y.: New City, 1985), pp. 93, 62.

38. Chiara Lubich, *Jesus, the Heart of His Message*, p. 68.

39. Theresa Margaret Redi, quoted in Bert Ghezzi, *Miracles of the Saints*, (Grand Rapids: Zondervan, 1996), p. 30.

40. *The Dialogue* of Saint Catherine, quoted in Ghezzi, p. 58.

41. Thomas Merton, quoted in Marc Foley, O.C.D., *The Love That Keeps Us Sane* (New York: Paulist, 2000), p. 60.

42. Frederick Faber, quoted in Foley, p. 63.

43. Thomas Howard, *Hallowed Be This House* (San Francisco: Ignatius, 1976), p. 26.

44. Donald Wuerl, *The Catholic Way: Faith for Living Today* (New York: Image, 2001), p. 293.

45. Edward Sri, *Men, Women and the Mystery of Love* (Cincinnati: Servant, 2007), p. 55.

46. Alice von Hildebrand, quoted in Sri, p. 84.

47. Søren Kierkegaard, *Works of Love*, Edward and Edna Hong trans. (New York: Harper, 1962), pp. 168–169.

48. Bonaventure, quoted in Rawley Myers, *The Saints Show Us Christ* (San Francisco: Ignatius, 1996), p. 126.

49. Henri J.M. Nouwen, *A Letter of Consolation* (New York: Harper One, 1982), p. 16.

50. John Paul II, quoted in Michael E. Gaitley, M.I.C., *Consoling the Heart of Jesus* (Stockbridge, Mass.: Marian, 2011), p. 58.

51. Augustine of Hippo, quoted in John Eldridge *The Journey of Desire* (Nashville: Thomas Nelson, 2000), p. 134.

52. Louis Evely, *Joy* (New York: Herder and Herder, 1968), p. 81.

53. C.S. Lewis, quoted in Clyde S. Kilby, ed., *A Mind Awake: An Anthology of C.S. Lewis* (New York: Harcourt Brace Jovanovich, 1968), p. 198.

54. Adrienne Von Speyer, *The Countenance of the Father*, Dr. David Kipp, trans. (San Francisco: Ignatius, 1997), p. 53.

55. Malcolm Muggeridge, *Jesus the Man Who Lives* (New York: Harper & Row, 1975), p. 71.

56. Desmond Tutu, quoted in Henri J.M. Nouwen, *Home Tonight* (New York: Doubleday, 2009), p. 41.

57. Julian of Norwich, quoted in Henri J.M. Nouwen, *Home Tonight*, p. 89.

58. Francois Fénelon, *Let Go* (New Kensington, Pa.: Whitaker, 1973), p. 37.

59. M. Basilea Schlink, *Realities* (Grand Rapids: Zondervan, 1966), pp. 89–90.

60. J.I. Packer, *Knowing God* (Downers Grove, Ill.: InterVarsity, 1973), p. 124.

61. John of the Cross, quoted in Chervin, p. 130.

62. Francis de Sales, quoted in Bernard Bangley, ed., *Living Love, A Modern Edition of Treatise on The Love of God* (Brewster, Mass.: Paraclete, 2003), p. 98.

63. Thérèse of Lisieux, quoted in Cavnar, pp. 48–49.

64. Bernard of Clairvaux, quoted in Ralph Martin, *The Fulfillment of All Desire: A Guidebook for the Journey to God Based on the Wisdom of the Saints* (Steubenville, Ohio: Emmaus Road, 2006), p. 257.

65. Francis de Sales, *Introduction to the Devout Life*, Allan Ross, ed. and trans. (Mineola, N.Y.: Dover, 2009), p. 161.

66. Mother Teresa of Calcutta, quoted in Jaya Chaliha, ed., *The Joy in Loving: A Guide to Daily Living* (New York: Viking, 1997), p. 72.

67. Marie de Mandat-Grancey, quoted in *The Life of Sister Marie De Mandat-Grancey and Mary's House in Ephesus*, Reverend Matthew Bartulica (Charlotte, N.C.: Tan, 2010), p. 29.

68. Paul Johnson, quoted in *Render Unto Caesar: Serving the Nation by Living Our Catholic Beliefs in Political Life*, Charles J. Chaput (New York: Random House, 2009), p. 72.

69. Fulgence of Ruspe, quoted in *A Dictionary of Quotes From the Saints*, Paul Thigpen (Ann Arbor, Mich.: Servant, 2001), p. 135.

70. Raphaela Mary, quoted in Francis W. Johnston, ed., *The Voice of the Saints: Counsels from the Saints to Bring Comfort and Guidance in Daily Living* (Rockford, Ill.: Tan, 1986), p. 27.

71. Dorothy Day, quoted in *Meet Dorothy Day, Champion of the Poor*, Woodeene Koenig-Bricker (Ann Arbor, Mich.: Servant, 2002), p. 60.

72. C.S. Lewis, quoted in *The Business of Heaven: Daily Readings from C.S. Lewis*, Walter Hooper, ed. (New York: Harvest, 1984), p. 160.

73. Thomas à Kempis, *The Imitation of Christ* (New York: Doubleday, 1955), p. 84.

74. Peter Julian Eymard, quoted in John Hardon, ed., *The Treasury of Catholic Wisdom* (San Francisco: Ignatius, 1987), p. 584.

75. Catherine de Hueck Doherty, quoted in *Grace in Every Season*, Mary Achterhoff (Ann Arbor, Mich.: Servant, 1992), p. 28.

76. Francis Xavier Nguyen Van Thuan, *Five Loaves & Two Fish* (Boston: Pauline, 1997), p TK.

77. Simone Weil, quoted in Donald De Marco, *The Heart of Virtue* (San Francisco: Ignatius, 1996), p. 37.

78. Ambrose of Milan, quoted in Claire Russell, *Glimpses of the Church Fathers* (New York: Scepter, 1994), p. 190.

79. Thérèse of the Child Jesus, quoted in John P. McClernon, ed. *Sermon in a Sentence: A Treasury of Quotations on the Spiritual Life* (San Francisco: Ignatius, 2002), p. 98.

80. Charles de Foucauld, quoted in Jean-Jacques Antier, *Charles De Foucauld* (San Francisco: Ignatius, 1999), p. 161.

81. Cardinal Christoph Schönborn, *My Jesus, Encounter Christ in the Gospel* (San Francisco: Ignatius, 2002), pp. 137–138.

82. David E. Rosage, *Follow Me* (Ann Arbor, Mich.: Servant, 1982), p. 231.

83. David E. Rosage, *Follow Me*, p. 233.

84. Benedict XVI, *Saved in Hope* (Ijamsville, Md.: The Word Among Us, 2007), pp. 10–11.

85. Benedict XVI, *God Is Love* (Boston: Pauline, 2006), p. 17.

86. Peter Julian Eymard, quoted in *The Real Presence: Eucharistic Meditations* (Cleveland, Ohio: Emmanuel, 1938), p. 4.

87. Faustina Kowalska, quoted in Michael E. Gaitley, M.I.C., *Consoling the Heart of Jesus* (Stockbridge, Mass.: Marian, 2010, p. TK.

88. Maurice Zundel, *With God in Our Daily Life* (Montreal: Editions Paulines, 1993), p. 114.

89. Maximilian Kolbe, quoted in Brother Anthony Josemaria, F.T.I., ed., *The Blessed Virgin Mary in England* (Bloomington, Ind.: iUniverse, 2008), p. 377.

90. Faustina Kowalska, quoted in Sophia Michalenko, C.M.G.T., *The Life of Faustina Kowalska: The Authorized Biography* (Cincinnati: Servant, 1999), p. 141.

91. Elizabeth Leseur, *The Secret Diary of Elizabeth Leseur* (Manchester, N.H.: Sophia, 2002), p. 173.

92. Leseur, p. 150.

93. Padre Pio, quoted in Eileen Dunn Bertanzetti, ed., *Listening to God with Padre Pio* (Huntington, Ind.: Our Sunday Visitor, 2011), p. 50.

94. Dogmatic Constitution on the Church, 42, quoted in Leonard

Foley, O.F.M., *Saint of the Day* (Cincinnati: St. Anthony Messenger Press, 1994), p. 41.

95. Pedro Arrupe, S.J., quoted in James Martin, S.J., ed., *My Life with the Saints* (Chicago: Loyola, 2006), p. 105.

96. Catherine de Hueck Doherty, quoted in Robert Ellsberg, ed., *All Saints, Daily Reflections of Saints, Prophets and Witnesses for Our Time* (New York: Crossroad, 1998), p. 352.

97. Pope John Paul II, quoted in Christopher West, *Good News About Sex and Marriage* (Cincinnati: Servant, 2000), p. 45.

98. Père Jacques Bunol, quoted in Ellsberg, *All Saints*, p. 51.

99. Francis de Sales, quoted in Ellsberg, *All Saints*, p. 43.

100. St. Jean Marie Vianney, quoted in the *Catechism of the Catholic Church*, 2658.

101. Peter Chrysologus, quoted in John Bartunek, L.C., ed., *The Better Part* (North Haven, Conn.: Circle, 2007), p. 220.

102. Theresa Margaret of the Sacred Heart, quoted in Bartunek, p. 432.

103. Mother Teresa of Calcutta, quoted in Gwen Costello, ed., *Spiritual Gems from Mother Teresa* (Mystic, Conn.: Twenty-Third, 2008), p. 9.

104. Father Engelmar Unzeitig, quoted in Robert Ellsberg, *The Saints' Guide to Happiness: Practical Lessons in the Life of the Spirit*, p. 101.

105. John of the Cross, quoted in Maurice Zundel, *The Gospel Within* (Sherbrooke, Quebec: Éditions Paulines, 1993), p. 124.

106. Cardinal Leon Joseph Suenens, *Christian Life Day by Day* (Westminster, Md.: Newman, 1961), p. 20.

107. William Blake, quoted in Ellsberg, *The Saints' Guide to Happiness*, p. 79.

108. Corrie Ten Boom, quoted in Robert Ellsberg, *Blessed Among All Women: Women Saints, Prophets, and Witnesses for Our Time* (New York: Crossroads, 2005), p. 206.

109. Catherine of Siena, quoted in Patricia Mary Vinje, *Praying with Catherine of Siena* (Ijamsville, Md.: The Word Among Us, 1990), p. 42.

110. Katharine Drexel, quoted in Leo Luke Marcello, *15 Days of Prayer with Saint Katharine Drexel* (Liguori, Mo.: Liguori, 2002), p. 87.

111. Georges Vanier, quoted in Ann Ball, *Faces of Holiness: Modern Saints in Photos and Words, Volume 2* (Huntington, Ill.: Our Sunday Visitor, 2001), p. 140.

112. Augustine of Hippo, quoted in Martin H. Manser, *The Westminster Collection of Christian Quotations* (Louisville, Ky.: Westminster John Knox, 2001), p. 185.

113. Romano Guardini, *The Living God* (Manchester, N.H.: Sophia Institute, 1985), pp. 41–42.

114. Basil Hume, O.S.B., quoted in Teresa de Bertodano, ed., *Cardinal Basil Hume: In My Own Words* (London: Hodder & Stoughton, 1999), p. 68.

16. Thomas à Kempis, quoted in *The Imitation of Jesus Christ: A Study of Its Spirituality*, Pierre Pourrat, available at http://www.ewtn.com/library/SPIRIT/IMITSPIR.TXT.

116. Teresa of Avila, quoted in Ronda Chervin, ed., *Spiritual Friendship, Darkness and Light* (Boston: St. Paul, 1992), p. 78.

117. Louis-Marie de Montfort, *The Love of Eternal Wisdom*, A. Somers, S.M.M., trans. (Bayshore, N.Y.: Montfort, 1986), p. 1.

118. Ann Shields, S.G.L., *Fire in My Heart* (Ann Arbor, Mich.: Servant, 1988), p. 28.

119. Pope Pius XII, quoted in *Catholic Saints Prayer Book*, Donna-Marie Cooper O'Boyle (Huntington, Ind.: Our Sunday Visitor, 2008), p. 55.

120. Catherine of Siena, quoted in Cooper O'Boyle, p. 25.

About the Author

Debra Herbeck has worked extensively in youth and women's ministry for the past thirty years. She is the director of the Renewal Ministries School of Catholic Bible Study and the newsletter editor for Renewal Ministries. Her books include *Safely Through the Storm: 120 Reflections on Hope* and *Firmly on the Rock: 120 Reflections on Faith*.